Opening Ceremony
© 2024 Laura Marie Marciano

ISBN: 978-1-988355-60-3

Published by Metatron Press
Montreal, Quebec
www.metatron.press

Printed in Canada

First printing

Art: Carly Jean Andrews

OPENING CEREMONY

LAURA MARIE MARCIANO

METATRON PRESS

for melo

FOURTH, I

I find you in the basement of a ranch house
touching the dirt bikes with a beer in your hand

A sort of dance in a rural ballroom, asking
for a ride past goats with fluorescent eyes,

hand-thrown fireworks,
milkweed

The people here are thin of spirit, and they
throw their bodies outwards like stop lights

You look to me for help, but am I
of these people, too

Your throat is tangled, New Yorker
in waxy black denim, somewhere
between too quiet and never stops

Forehead tattoo like a burning halo
in a hollow town

Is this where decency has been restored
a vacuum of better not and don't know better

                              And what happens if
they call you handsome when your mouth
is closed

I think of your nephew who said he had flowers
in his yard
                    but they belonged to the landlord

The air is between summer and fall even though
it is only July— we can tell by the fire in our noses

Someone asks if we will move out here, have children

You say yes, and then no, before the blue steel barn

and our eyes catch smoke

OPENING CEREMONY

In an Airbnb in San Juan, we are *trying*—

Removing track pants in pale morning

Near coral, rough tides after dinner

I am tempted to stay wide with you here,

Floating like frog and scorpion in pool

LED lights on skin, swift kick in the chin from a sibling

What if I stopped mentioning my too small mouth?
Placed an apricot inside, in my too small house,
which you hoped would be bigger!

We are casual texters, former indie scum

Caught in security mirror, once the sad clowns

of Tumblr, aware that you can be

a mom and still be a dumb bitch

I am a monster next to my husband

Chiseled-face like a prism and my pinkish

skin in this sun reminds me of trains, or

middle management, nothing pretty like him

I text my aesthetic nurse for advice

She suggests botox, lip and cheek fillers,

a weekend away in Stowe for $200 a night

I ask myself

Laura, haven't I punished you enough? A child in this economy?
I remember you pressed against me and touched my heart
I remember you placed sapphires in my wide, listening ears
I remember we knew the insurrection was a staged event
That we prayed for job security

I get that we are not the same, that we are older now

That insurance companies have hired drones to spy on us

That we have slept on basement couches in second homes

I am faking it, too, you see, in this pool in San Juan

I am wondering when my womb will be full with our baby

I want to stay open and tight and keep you around, *baby*

Until the salt lick stops the horse, and the ground light

near palm trees   softens this curve of our lives

THE THOUGHT OF OWNING A POOL, ABSURD

POOL BLUE

This leaf in pool water is a kind of mercy
a spring in recess, the thought of
owning a pool, absurd

In the ring light I kneel on bruises
bladder full, N95 mask, over-lined lips

My neighbors by a bigger TV
that takes both women to carry it upstairs

I am having these doubts,
how the weather can't decide its mood or

>   about the racoon outside my window, local news,
>   missed fertile windows, government checks
>   that never arrive

If you ask me why I am so forlorn, I might pause or say
I think lime green will be in again this summer

Pink cheeks filled with a kind of pride
To talk of summer, as if we still know what
each other feels like

CREAM PIE IN 2016

The filmmaker asked what Monica and I
Wished to capture and I say a porn because
The flirtation of platonic bonds imploding
Still excited a boy like him— all neon energy
When we pretend to watch the Super Bowl

The body is the silver lining of nothing sent across
Class, science, zip codes, politics, or I am
Most delicate when caught suddenly in your gaze
The male-gaze, the filmmaker-gaze, slow touch past Judeo-Islam
Food cart in midtown, and we all laughed, took selfies

Weather grew warm and I was obsessed with data
The days post discard are hardest then again
I did not think you looked as hot when you begged
But now ten days after no contact I remember how
Sexy you are and how I have become unsexed

Spending hours speaking with Angie Antkinson
A YouTube life-couch, about narcissistic abuse
And someone is going to tell me that they didn't
Think a woman so intelligent could be so dumb
As if we are still playing that childhood game *fuck/marry/kill*

The leisure and pleasure of poetry is minimal
Take for instance the bag that incriminates me
When I walk by your place of work on Tuesday
Aqua blue and faux fur and at the same time the
Ocean somewhere in California just touched a spot of skin

On a body, on salt, on the marina and coral reefs
I cried at work for the first time today and
Thought of stocks and bonds and Katy who asked me if
Our freak president suffered from N.P.D like you do
And I love you, anyway, write whole books about you

This entropy of womanhood, of fat bodies
Chubby girl porn you searched on my brother's
Computer and the anger of separation like how much
Can I love you, I think of your sister, and I want to ask

If your mother is longing for you and the other Laura
And Emily and Jenny and Rachel and Camoghne
Until we all burst into shattering glass as victims
Of your perfect, Turbo-Tax, mnml.la, E-Trade, CBD
Wifey Wakes to Cream-Pie addicted to boyhood body

Not like the filmmaker, but not dissimilar either

The tired hetero metaphor is crossed with debility
I bring out misogyny in even the most woke of men
In my tight thing near the restaurant, in my wet bottoms
And I was getting F.O.M.O that my girlfriends had
Abandoned feminist thought without me

The pierce of nothing in ear is a real sound and I can prove it

YEARS LATER

The filmmaker gives a speech at my wedding, farm style
bouquets on bare tables

RED MOON ECLIPSE WITH MARS VISIBLE

I missed the latest retrospective at
DIA Beacon and the red moon is
surfacing too much for a kid with my
salary to manage

Look I know I promised I would not
collect the mortals from the gutter but
I just can't help myself

On a Tuesday I wake up a
daughter and a mother in a
childless garden

With two full-time, non-tenured jobs
the milk before the cow
Could I be more of a clown?

A performance in class-passing is
exhausting

I lay down in the office

I feel grateful   I do that now

COMMODITY

This is bad for me
to be so close to this

Giving up $300
to turn eggshells with tongue

We suffer so much for our art

My angels all have vaginal infections
Who knew they could be so dumb
the ones who carry lavender
in between shoulder blades

Everyone was crying this week

I am a wilted dove
An orchid in bulb
A failed market strategy

My skin won't respond
to Juvéderm injections

The dean won't hire adjuncts
full-time

I've lived my whole life
in commercial deceit

The way we liked holidays
Whole families gathered with
pumpkins, the way we built malls
as public space

I wanted to build grand teal chapels when
all I was offered was unemployment

the tragedy of inter-class marriage or

What can we learn from our peers?

ON GRIEF

It is daylight savings in LA again
and porn won't load on phone
or in the heavy cheat of Spring
I see a boy leave the theater
when two men kiss

My fashion icon teaches me to
sniff directly up my nose,
tiny beads, she says
and in the orange
head-rush I find
conceit for time
for erotica
            plush
this melancholia of drinks after work
my pride falling with my fortunes

Outside murmurs in DTLA
I didn't expect so many pastels
A woman weeps over a marble statue
in her mint cotton joggers
Now I'm the one to go when
I see my own self in another

TWEEN SUPREME

As good as a mossy summer scent and gasoline
I introduce you to Acqua di Parma but you
perfer Sol de Janeiro

Open as a raincloud, Natalia, strawberry blonde
Blush and bold with your Stanley Cup in *pool blue*

Shein cart, spring haul, short dress, Converse
short-shorts, Nike pro-tech, Glossier balm.com

And then your dusty ass son hi-fives her
at her volleyball game in Kingston

That crazy text she sent the family chat
about needing to date, and didn't we
all believe in love?

She wants to be an oceanographer
and study dolphins

My first born niece, perfect
as a blue-chip investment
that her daddy can not afford

I will buy Brandy Melville to insure her
Tell the uncles to step back from her feet

Hide her mid-house from view, 'Return
to Tiffany' on wrist, wash her shame

in familial water, french nails done, too

GIRL DINNER

I am so sorry that I have no thirds to offer you
dangling like a loose dollar at the chaotic
Versace sample sale in Chelsea, the perfect
flâneur

I am a masochist, you know this of course
I want to make you happy at my expense
I want an Oro Blanco grapefruit, half an avocado,
tuna fish in olive oil, low-fat flax seed crackers
A perfect bite

I want you to want me, lead me through tall trees
send blue valentines, stand up tall, nod at company,
listen to Reich for 18 Musicians
be a hot mom

When I ask a friend for help getting
an interview at her company
and she sidecocks at my outfit

I overhear the hot moms
having hot mom talks
about how hot they are and in turn
how much they deserve it all

Too bad I am predisposed to stay poor

PRETTY RICKY

I heard they called my man
Pretty Ricky in Bed-Stuy, summer of 2002

Honey brown contacts,
and somewhere else, mine were blue

Pretty boy, doin' pretty good thangs
Thighs smooth under cool, public waters

LUAR, MARSHMALLOW!

Is fluid thin-bodied and lush a captured Fiorucci angel
or Baz Luhrmann's Romeo through fish tank We exchange
money for attention colorway of aqua burnt orange pale
pink— touch tongues with YouTube beauty bloggers over a
summer stew as if it's how we learned to breathe *In the Bag*
Episode 40 *British Vogue* with Kali Uchis in baby blue knee
socks gray pleated skirt gray sweater vest and she pulled out
a Game Boy Hello Kitty Covid mask and roll-on with citrine
crystals from a translucent blue Chanel with gold double c
I really got into that the way I love Luar too it's how I feel about
you too and when you stood against double white doors shirtless
my white Ana bag around neck in afternoon light What did I do
in this life to share space with marble statue the way jeans sit on
your narrow hips 6'2" frame how you cook eggs for my parents
My Heart Will Go On on Tivoli Radio Each New York sports team
tattoo on arm even though you do not like sports or play sports
An original hipster that the white girls followed when they arrived in
your neighborhood in 2010 and I was the last of them Walking with
you in Prospect Park you nod at this man near the dumpster who
thought you might be cruising too

ABEL

When the boy gave Jesus

seven loaves and a few small fish

      he hauled ass and got them fed

I am in awe of the mundane
spill of change   periodical visits
from the darkest three hours of your life
Head split on concrete   or how

you know how to sew because
your grandmother taught you
out of embarrassment, you told her
of the holes in your own clothes

the peach-flavored hustle
Like yours, Cain,
or your brother

when he flew from a Range Rover
into a tree and still visited with us
weeks later to give his blessing

Reminds me that you and he

Irish-twins   came from the dirt

without mention of the flowers

ON LIVE-STREAM, YOU IN THE GAS STATION LIGHT, 2019

It's not going to make sense to the father
who sent me to parochial school to avoid
this outcome

But now you and he are pumping gas over
Christmas

My boyfriend, wearing a royal purple do-rag
In vain, or for vanity, ashamed of the day his hair
fell out

My boyfriend, wearing a belt made of silver bullets
On livestream, in the gas station
light

Sampson have we cut
Carmelo have we seared

I was not convinced until he stumbled
through the door in November, FedEx
uniform, boots heavier than his frame

I was not convinced until he held
laptop above head so I could view
Tangerine more clearly— hear
Sin-Dee's vocal fry

I wish all of you could have seen
portraits June took of my grandmother
ornamenting the inner violence of
Europe, wool skirt suit with tight red
hem

How the portraits are regal like my
boyfriend, lineage sewn in the wool-
blood and soot left on condom

How our bodies link like horseshoes in
a pony show we didn't start

How after we had sex, we tossed it out

AT DUSK ON THE EVE OF OUR CEREMONY, 2022

On the eve of our ceremony, we are two
Bodies likely to never touch again, and
Two mothers, one on herbal tranquilizers and
The other greeting a caterer, hold us somehow -
Every whisper is a crash on my ear, all blue
At dusk, farmhouse wood stairs and hydrangea

How quaint the sight of spiders on the porch,
Green leafy umbrella above New England breeze
Your brother's Range Rover wrecked back in
New York, his four children who we have called
To stand beside us, safely inside, but still
Her fast, anxious tongue won't quit

I liked the way the house looked against pale blue,
Dark bend and two friends cake on Too-Faced
Multi-sculpting concealer and wear synthetic slips
Smile when I enter full and befogged by their
Kindness, near sand, near the Devil's Slide
On roads lined with low light and August brush

After the silent touch of forced hand and
The silent death of our names and wardrobes
Into lace white dress and kilt, you will say
Goodbye to poverty forever and for that
Matter cash payments, domestic and whole
In our trauma bond, in our shared debt

We will have to build a new house but the tools
Are askew, one whose hands work and
Are hardened by labor and me who has only
Extended the bulb of my orchid in theory, only
Carried boxes when moving to the top floor
Now ready to send your boy money through JPay

When I met you you were a viral fry thief
Walked into McDonalds and the working
Girls let you take them all, on video and
You worked, too, at a liquor warehouse
Facetimed me on midday break, pale skin
Against your screen, in my pink satin towel

When you met me, face plump with Hoola
Bronzer and gold, completing an advanced
Degree in poetry, letting broke hot girls sleep
In my living room, just learning about Adderall
Scooped in chrome nail, white IKEA bookcase
That let the light through while you penetrate me

I am brilliant they say, but you are
Adored, who has gathered, sold and slung
Blow folded pizza boxes, protected young
Chickenheads in the street, climbed hills
Passed used needles and glass, to come home
To a tapestry of casual addicts and fools

On our second meeting you brought me
A prism, and one for hot Monica too, and
Light refracted in my chest, because
What if all that Feist and Sufjan I loved
Meant your coat wasn't lifted from H&M
And that the prism wasn't stolen, too

I have followed the probability of success
Two wounded birds from different flight patterns
Cross in a memorial sky, a sacrificial, short
Haired boomer thankful for any marriage at all
All that liberal education and mental illness aside
To be without sin now, barring petty crime at our altar

Now dusk is a whisper, and children from the car
Have finally arrived, stretched out, stand beside us
Little gold chains, and daisy chains, and
Black curls and red braids and little
Bells on string and then ok what
Kind of trouble is this but good trouble

Like a plot of antiques on the bed sheets
A personal injury check   uncashed

POEM FOR OUR WEDDING

Say it with pale peach highway florals
as seen on South Conduit Avenue in Queens

      between April and September
an unsuspected summer bloom, like a
      lone firework at dawn
Or the seven siblings we gained
when we shared their phone numbers

In a fever dream I carried a wounded bird
all the way up a withered mountain

         in return
          I found you

Are we called to the cloud on screen
or in the universe, the memorial of sky
     the December of June
honeysuckle   wire   flame

IT IS 2023

And my aesthetic nurse
is pregnant before me
Hot barbie pink vape
blowing air

FOURTH, II

This is someone else's good fortune

This is where we ask to not be seen

4th of July in Bed-Stuy, rainbow in puddled oil
and through rearview mirror I see you,
bright orange shirt, blue mouth, walk confidently

One cop makes a comment about how neatly you rolled up
says there's a warrant for your arrest (unpaid bike ticket)
You spend Independence Day in a holding cell

Eyes peel upon entering the thick air of morning
wild lone fireworks over nearby picnic grounds

The next day I record a poem at Carnegie Hall

AT MIDNIGHT, WHAT BODY

ASH WEED

I am so done with feeling
Xmas Amaryllis grow in places
where they do not belong

I am not quite enough for the
clinic— promoting myself again
after all insurance claims have been made

In Casablanca I wait for livestock
to come through luxe doors for
thighs to grow fat through
absorption

My killer is not going
to be invited to this
ornamenting party
and I am blue daisies
casting oh's wide in anointment

Now that they've gone
I am free to torch down the valley
La spiaggia of pure purple,
small neck in hand

VINCE GUARLDI TRIO ON BLUETOOTH, TRYING TO CONCEIVE

I feel like rage

And nostalgia

Keep me up

Visions of Verona

Leonardo and Judas

Countrymen

Or my 45-inch bust

In a sample size

Angels swell, burst

Atlantic Surge

Soaks through

My Fiorucci t-shirt

I flood the grass

Fiori di Napoli

Bloom in the driveway

What if this body

-Is Broken

And I tried to tell you

We are parked

On Graham Avenue

Greensleeves

Plays on Bluetooth

Hitachi Magic Wand

Softly over

Bell bottoms

Oversized hair clips

Black velvet

Frustrated

But hopeful, you

Asleep

What if we play

Violin, sew satin

Details on handmade skirts

Instead of always

Doing what

We do

All we have now

A temple

To impulse buys

A marathon of

OPK strips, timed

Intercourse

How I wanted

Net-A-Porter

CRISPR baby

Oysters and wine

Tan legs

Holographic

Handbag

Yellow diamond

White press on nails

Pasta

Headlights

False lashes

Jacuzzi light

White rug

For dinner

I am imitating

Never look at me

She went back

I throw a pool party

Should we just

Men

Square

To an abuser

For fat women

Give up

How they write

During pleasure

Not ok, but ok

Only

For now

I wish I could

Vince Guaraldi Trio

Flirt with the women

In the late summer office

Tell them all about

At the year end party

BOMB ROSE WATER

It is April and I am wearing Tommy Girl which though
only 35 dollars is a 5-star scent in *Perfumes: The Guide 2018*
rated by top noses top note of apple blossoms like a
hot tea in summer but you prefer the bomb rose water on our
sheets Santa Maria novella an 800 year-old formula made
originally by monks in the hills outside Florence Italy
Your long limbs are wrapped around a Boba Tea-shaped
plushy pillow and I do believe in a nirvana that does
not require one to leave the house like ever and with no
effort just lying in bed or on the couch and then what does
it mean to lie and not work at least for an afternoon or
whenever you come home from seeing certain friends and
the iron of high heat in housing projects is on your clothes
intoxicating really it is a sexy scent that reminds me of when
you first took my photo on the floor near a mirrored chest
Our wedding bouquet on bedpost smells so faintly of rotted
peonies and the dirt we rolled in near Stony Kill Falls on our
first anniversary I feel the boulder of despair shrink a little
when I think of Saugerties in spring and fill our hands with
sweet clementines or bitter Duchesse d'Angouleme pear the
watermelon dole aftertaste of last summer or that piña colada
with candy cherry scent you gave me in the car on the long
road to Loiza sitting out the window while Ava Maria played
off Bluetooth and it's ok if no one gets us really

I SHOULD FEEL BLESSED

To be an auntie to nearly ten children
body intact sour grape sapphire earrings
from TraxNYC your Apple watch, your
Ombré Leather Tom Ford cologne

And still we give to these kids their bright
open gasps video games with Tio
dress-up baskets, ski trips

And still what is our body for

is it for this

TIJUANA AT 5 IN THE AFTERNOON

A man and his son ride on horseback
past an Amazon warehouse built above
El Cerro de las Abejas in an image shared
online

The violent juxtaposition of
late capitalism tragic art

Back home I think about how messy
I keep this house, used pregnancy tests
behind couch

Say it with flowers, I say it
more to say

AT MIDNIGHT WHAT BODY DOES THIS OCEAN NOT DESERVE

I am anxious

covered in Sol de Janeiro body oil

      I have not swam all of July

Five months pregnant and I find out my
contract was not renewed through an
automated email from university
computing services

A violet flower blooms

What have I gotten myself into

WATER DEATH

A dry body will not decompose

Or in July violet sedum bloom

In her driveway

Pool water soaks through my

knitted-skirt

My mother whose shame

I share, once too loved pools

In New Jersey, emerged

No echo or taunts from

Summer boys and

What body does not deserve

To feel air on all limbs

In air the body decays

Three times faster than water

When I need a dream fulfilled, I eat

Yellow tomato, figs and ricotta

Tortellini in pesto

My mother, pearly in sun

Has not swum in twenty years

If not dreaming, than searching

Amazon for a swimsuit that covers

Head to toe

Bacteria in-gut, chest cavity

Balloons with gas

The body now floats,

Decays, a viking funeral

Before death

But I remember you on the beach

I am five, illuminating sounds in

White-pink shells, green apples in palm
We peed in sand while Nonna called you fat

Cold water encourages adipocere

The more flesh, the more foam

We are intact, recognizable skeletons

After we drown, though once great swimmers

The pool now covered in ice

Christmas fish in our bellies

If I could have maimed summer boys,

Winterized Amalfi and Long Beach Island

For you   I would

At midnight

                    what body does this ocean not deserve

25 PARADE PLACE

I must speak kindly to my neighbors

I watch them play tennis, vote for Biden
Close the door on you

after you moved in with me
Leave trash at our door

I wish we could just do something to become less poor

Make those assholes pay for telling my landlord
about your forehead tattoo

Build a farmhouse in New Paltz, lock ankles under
plastic card tables, sell hand-sewn tablecloths online

Win at Sundance for our queer little film

But all we do?

Bring free samples home from the farmer's market
A small thrill

STAND ON YOUR EXPERIENCE

Until your boss hires her husband over you or

how I wish the way my words sounded was what my

face looked like

CARMELO

I smear you on my chest in the heat Anything
I ask for you give to me I was inside of a coat
against a door near roof dwellers of Bushwick
Houses Now holding me in tropical waters in
Newport day spas your hands and the way work
made them You run yourself into the ground I lay
down Who else can drive a semi through a storm
and sew a perfect hem? Yet heart of green keeps
me up! Boss has a crush on you The waitress in
Greenpoint leaves photo on your phone-Shadows
at parties who follow you into stalls Niqua always
calling you and asking for a ride in my damn car—
it causes me fever! I also don't get why I can't peer
into your eyeballs literally two black orbs like blown
glass looking back at me on our Joy Bird pink velvet
couch I've seen so much inside of this multitudes and
spirals Like a feeding trough or the place that Italian cats
are held by friendly neighbors who leave out sweet milk
Just like the cat I fed at six in our front yard or the way
you protect me even when I leave wet towels on the
floor Have you not saint lips and holy hands too?

FOURTH, III

In July, your sister held me and said she liked
my yellow highlights, asked me what I might do
if a man, after twelve years, treated me like
he didn't have a daughter

I told her we must already know each other
broken outside a 70th and Beach Street apartment
Long Island Sound salt in our noses — a slight breeze

Flesh is not currency when your birth is a siren
cold before the sale, or I wish I was a pale peach flower
rolled in cement here in Queens

Now the sound of a tween girl held on the ground
near a Honda Civic, with no insurance, interrupts us

My God, where is the rose gold hot tub for Tina!
She deserves to be rich anywhere
Stay home by a pool, sleep

The irony is that we don't swim anymore and
Your sister is shocked when you serve me a plate

A friend texts to ask if her man would leave
if she can't lose the baby weight?

I hold Tina a little bit tighter
champagne on our breath

What are we celebrating
when untouchable feelings are under siege

AFTER, OPEN

This dead bird was moving for hours like
God himself thrown it to earth in a fitful rage

I was once the perfect size in the Florentine countryside
Where my writing teacher groped me in 2007

Still I have the audacity to speak at all because
Speculative literature runs faster than weight gain

I remember Paris with my friends, café in
downpour, a tangerine filled bread at dusk

I remember Venice with my brother, glitter in
Our train seats, a vomit smell on my arm

I remember Los Angeles with Holiday, in a
Parking lot, reading poems against a fence of roses

I remember Cobble Hill with Omega, driving
With no purpose, watching you cry on the phone

I remember your kid said I couldn't live in the
Shared brownstone because I had none of my own

Now a wish of our limitations and endless bickering
Real Aurora Fonseca, a name we could both agree upon

I am face down in a pool, no news crew, warm air is
West of us, rolling grapes on flesh to feel something

Sublet June to January to save money for this event
I have to retake the NIPT due to low fetal fraction

My father asks, *what's that?*
He reminds you of your boss at Fedex
Suck my dick

Millennial pink and a mandatory vaccine, thousands of
monitoring appointments with a flippant doctor and now

Anoint our baby with all the luxuries we can imagine
Bugaboo stroller, doc-a-tot, winter staycation
Nonna says even the richest people can be poor

What thy bless, no man can curse
What thy bless, no man can curse

A purple light from the toilet stares up at us,

a positive test
I piss on the floor

IN AN AIRBNB IN SAN JUAN

Then we met each other

Now older than all of our rapists at
least seven years and three oceans
— Primigrivada

American poor
American middle class

And we are recognized mirrorball
edgelords   failsons   pansies
a minor revolution online or outside
Party City

From Providence to Pulaski St. From
Liguria to Loiza

Aurora Borealis like the sky that
conceived your cousin
present tropical sober open
      waiting and what else can we do

with gratitude

ACKNOWLEDGEMENTS

Opening Ceremony, like my first collection (*Mall Brat*), is a poetic memoir, investigating the most recent decade of life.

Thank you to Wonder and Poetry Foundation for publishing earlier versions of Vince Guarladi Trio and Ash Weed. Thank you to NPR's Poetry Now for discussing Ash Weed with me.

Thank you to my dear friend Omega for getting me through.

To my mother Carol, an extraordinary love.

To my husband Carmelo, for making things feel new.

To all my friends and family for always supporting me.

Thank you to Carly Jean Andrews for her spectacular artwork.

Thank you to all the poets and artists I adore including Joselia Hughes, Ana Carrete, Holiday Black, Annie Rose Malamet, Dannielle Venne, Lenny Adler, Daniel Diaz, Ava Jarden, Anna Cornachan, June Canedo, Monica McClure, Camoghne Felix, Maya Martinez, Sylvia Vaccaro, Harry Burke, Rand Rosenberg, Carlos Cardona, Sophia de Baun, Matt Harvey, Sophia Giovannitti, Precious Okyomon, Sophia Le Fraga, Kate Durbin, Fo Venne, Natalia Marciano, and to my dear Peter Covino, who helped me start this book.

Thank you to Metatron Press and Ashley Obscura for believing in this work. Your efforts to champion new works into the world is admirable and needed and deserves many bouquets.

Laura Marie Marciano

Laura Marie Marciano is an author, educator, and media artist. She received her MFA from Brooklyn College in Performance and Interactive Media Arts, and her PhD in English and Creative Writing from the University of Rhode Island. Laura's first book of poetry, *Mice Brat*, was released in 2016, from Civil Coping Mechanism Press. Excerpts from this book appear in the Poetry Foundation's archive, along with poems that appear in *Opening Ceremony*. Marciano is a multimodal artist, whose writing and performance have been featured with NPR and Poetry's podcast Poetry Now! She has curated works of poetry and performance at MoMA PS1, Brooklyn Museum, and RISD Museum, and has given readings at many venues across the nation, including Brown University. Laura is also a production artist who has worked on films that have been celebrated by the TriBeca Film Festival, and Sundance Film Festival. In 2014, Laura started gemstone readings, a poetry and video art collective. Her most recent production under this label is an experimental meditation on trans parenthood, which premiered in 2024 at Out-FRONT Fest in NYC.

Laura has served as an assistant editor for Barrow Street Press, and the Ocean State Review, while receiving her PhD under Dr. Peter Covino. She has studied with poets CA Conrad and Fred Moten, and is an active member of the poetry community. She served as a visiting assistant professor in writing at Lehigh University, and currently a full-time lecturer in writing at SUNY's premiere campus, Stony Brook University.

She lives in Brooklyn with her husband Carmelo.